Living in a Town

Richard Spilsbury

www.heinemannlibrary.co.uk
Visit our website to find out more information about Heinemann Library books.

To order:
☎ Phone +44 (0) 1865 888066
📄 Fax +44 (0) 1865 314091
💻 Visit www.heinemannlibrary.co.uk

Edited by Charlotte Guillain and
  Catherine Veitch
Designed by Joanna Hinton-Malivoire
Original illustrations © Capstone Global Library
Illustrated by Joanna Hinton-Malivoire
Picture research by Elizabeth Alexander and
  Fiona Orbell
Originated by Dot Gradations Ltd
Printed in China by South China Printing Company Ltd

ISBN 978 0 431020 87 7 (hardback)
14 13 12 11 10
10 9 8 7 6 5 4 3 2 1

British Library Cataloguing in Publication Data
Spilsbury, Richard
Living in a town. – (Our local area)
910.9'1732-dc22
A full catalogue record for this book is available from the British Library.

Acknowledgements
We would like to thank the following for permission to reproduce photographs: Alamy pp. **11** (©NearTheCoast.com), **14** (© Photofusion Picture Library), **21** (© Dave Ellison), © Capstone Global Library Ltd. pp. **6**, **8**, **9**, **10** &**13** (Tudor Photography); Construction Photography p. **19** (© Michael Reinhard); Corbis pp. **4** & **5** (© London Aerial Photo Library), **18** (© David Turnley); Courtesy of Lesley Boddy/ bornyesterday.org.uk p. **16** & **17**; Photofusion Picture Library p. **12** (© Paula Solloway).

Cover photograph of Battle Town Centre, Sussex, UK reproduced with permission of Alamy (© PCL).

We would like to thank Rachel Bowles for her invaluable help in the preparation of this book.

Every effort has been made to contact copyright holders of material reproduced in this book. Any omissions will be rectified in subsequent printings if notice is given to the publisher.

All the Internet addresses (URLs) given in this book were valid at the time of going to press. However, due to the dynamic nature of the Internet, some addresses may have changed, or sites may have changed or ceased to exist since publication. While the author and publisher regret any inconvenience this may cause readers, no responsibility for any such changes can be accepted by either the author or the publisher.

Contents

Any words appearing in the text in bold, **like this**, are explained in the glossary.

What is a town?

Towns are places where hundreds or even thousands of people live and work. Towns are usually bigger than villages and smaller than cities. Use a road map or **atlas** to find your nearest towns.

This town was built on a river. One of the oldest parts is the castle. What other **features** can you spot and name?

Many towns started as small villages. They grew into bigger towns when more people moved there to live and work. Many towns were built near crossing places on rivers. People used the river water for drinking, cooking, and working **watermills**.

Town buildings

Towns have buildings where people live, work, buy what they need, and have fun. There are also buildings like **health centres** and schools. The centre of a town is usually the oldest part. Old buildings here may include a **town hall**, a church, grand houses, and rows of cottages.

The **town council**, who run the town, meet in the town hall.

town hall

6

Most towns have many different shops. The smaller ones are often all together on streets in the town centre. Large shops, such as supermarkets, may be on the edge of towns.

Dani made a **bar chart** to show all the different shops in her town.

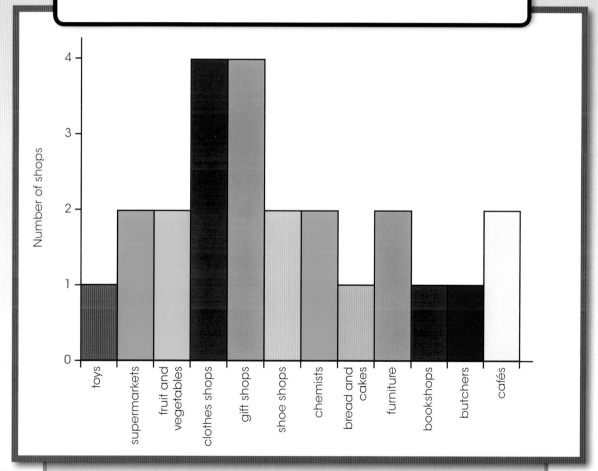

What kinds of shops are there in your local town? What has been missed out in Dani's list?

Town transport

Some towns are small enough to walk or cycle across. Other people catch one of the buses that go around the town. Most towns have a bus station. From here, people can travel out of town to other places.

Which places do you go to by bus?

Some fast trains whizz through town railway stations without stopping on their way between cities.

A town railway station may have two or more **platforms**. Local trains stop here to take people to other towns and cities. Taxis wait by stations to take people to exactly where they want to go from the station. Look at a map of your nearest town. How far is it from the bus or railway station to the places you like to go in the town?

Town jobs

Many people who live in a town also work in the town. Some people work together in **factories**. They use machines to help make things, such as pies or bread. Other people have jobs in chemists, banks, sport centres, or libraries.

Some people who live in towns have jobs making shoes, jewellery, or other items in their own small workshops.

Some people work in the **town hall.**
The **town council** meet there to sort
out problems and plan events.

Some people do jobs that help other people.
They may work in cafés making lunch for
people, or in garages mending people's cars.
You could take photos or draw pictures of the
different types of businesses in your local town.

Coming to town

People from villages often visit nearby towns. Some children come to town every day to go to school. People visit towns to buy things because towns have more shops than a village. Villagers may also come to town to have their eyes checked, or to see a doctor.

For many people, the nearest dentist is in a town.

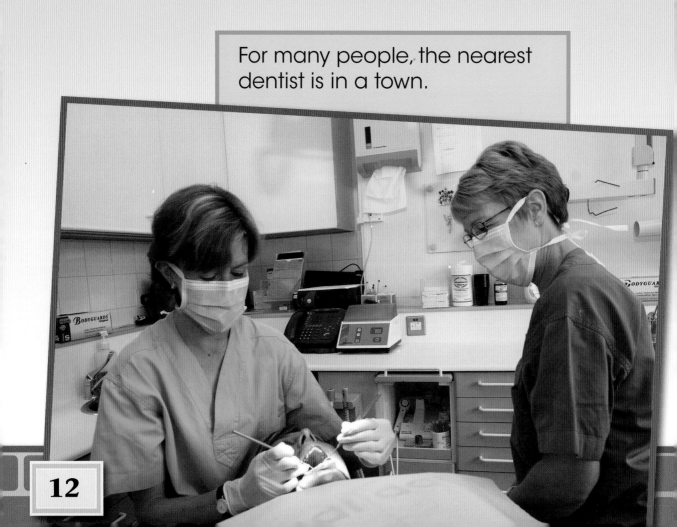

Many towns have special **markets** once a week or month. Markets have stalls selling things such as crafts or food. Farmers come to farmers' markets in towns to sell the food they grow. Visitors and people from towns like to buy local **products** at markets.

Are you near a market like this? What does it sell?

Things to do

There are usually more things to do in a town than in a village. In a town's **museum** you can learn about science, art, and history. In the town sport centre, people can swim and play other sports. Towns also have tennis courts and parks where people can play.

Many people join a gym in a town to exercise.

In a town theatre, people can join in with the **pantomime**.

When people are hungry in a town there is a choice of places to eat. Afterwards they might go to a cinema to watch a film. People may also go to halls, churches, or pubs to hear bands play music.

In the past

Towns change over time. People knock down some old buildings and build new ones. But some things stay the same. You can find old buildings like churches and **town halls** in most towns.

This is the same town as the one on the opposite page. What has changed over time?

In the past, many people in a town may have done the same job, such as coal mining or building cars. Today, many of these businesses may have closed down. Where would you go in a town to find out what jobs people used to do there in the past?

The circular red sign in this picture is a clue about transport changes in the town.

New towns

In some countries, poor people live in **shanty towns** when they come to a big city to work. In a shanty town, people sometimes make their houses from waste metal, wood, cardboard, and plastic. Shanty towns have few toilets, few doctors, and often have no electricity.

Think of three ways that a shanty town is different to where you live.

What buildings would you put in a new town? What kind of open spaces would you include?

In richer countries, town planners **design** new towns. They choose where to put buildings, such as schools, **health centres**, and shops. They plan where roads and paths for bicycles and **pedestrians** will go.

Improving towns

What do you like or dislike about your nearest town? Some people think towns would look nicer with more trees and gardens, and less litter. Some children might want to improve their town with a bigger swimming pool or a new skateboard park.

This town bicycle park is a place where lots of young people meet up to have fun on two wheels.

Lots of people drive cars, buses, and lorries in and out of towns. Traffic can be noisy, smelly, and dangerous. Some town centre streets are closed to traffic so they are safer and cleaner. Do you think this makes it easier or harder for people to visit towns?

About town

Maps help people find their way around towns. Use this map to follow the **route** from the bus station to the school. What buildings do you pass along the way?

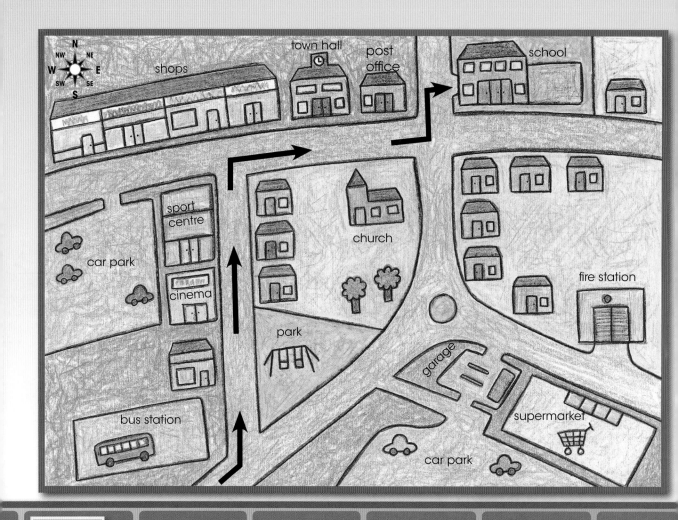

Glossary

atlas book containing maps and information about the world

bar chart type of graph where data, such as number of houses of a particular type, are shown as bars

design plan of how to build and lay out things in a space for a particular purpose

factory building where people make or process things to sell

features characteristics or appearance of an object or person

health centre clinic where sick people visit a nurse or doctor

market group of stalls selling things such as food or crafts

museum building in which people collect, study, and look after rare or interesting objects for other people to see

pantomime traditional, fun Christmas play based on a children's story, with costumes and singing

pedestrians people travelling by foot (walking)

platform raised structure passengers use to climb on or off a train

product something that is made or grown, usually to sell

route path of travel from one place to another

shanty town area of very poor housing often on the edges of a city

town council local government who runs a town

town hall building from where a local government runs a town

watermill building where grain is ground into flour using the power of water

Index

Find out more

Books to read

Belonging, Jeannie Baker (Walker Books, 2008)

The Town Mouse and the Country Mouse, Susanna Davidson and Jacqueline East (Usborne Publishing, 2007)

Websites

A Vision of Britain through Time
www.visionofbritain.org.uk/index.jsp
Visit this website to discover how your local town has changed through history.

Ordnance Survey – Get-a-Map
www.ordnancesurvey.co.uk/oswebsite/getamap/
This site provides OS maps that can be printed or copied. Get one for the town near where you live.